FINALLY: THE GOLF SHORT GAME'S
SIMPLE SECRET

An incredibly simple, effective and "easy to do" method
to significantly improve your short game that
is almost too good to be true

J. F. TAMAYO • 132 Photographs

"To the readers of my first book, FINALLY: The Golf Swing's Simple Secret. Thanks to your interest in my teaching methods and great reviews you gave me, I felt I had the duty to share with you, as well as with any other golfer interested in taking his game to a higher level, my latest and amazing discoveries I was lucky to find, which I am very confident will dramatically improve your short game." - J F TAMAYO

FINALLY: THE GOLF SHORT GAME'S SIMPLE SECRET
COPYRIGHT © 2016 JUAN F TAMAYO

FIRST EDITION
ISBN-13: 978-1539973072
ISBN-10: 1539973077

CONTENTS

☺ Correct

☹ Incorrect

1. ACKNOWLEDGEMENTS

Perhaps because golf is a such a difficult sport to improve and so frustrating at times, I have developed a passion for finding new and easier ways of doing a better golf swing. This has certainly helped me become a better player throughout the years.

It is also fair to say that the vast majority of ideas that come to my mind don't work for more than a few rounds. Nevertheless, I have also learned that the few ideas or concepts that end up working are worth the effort and have the potential of significantly improving any players' golf game, regardless of his age, gender or playing ability.

For this reason I would like to thank my kids, María, Juan Felipe and Santiago. Thanks to them, it has been possible to filter those great ideas that not only have worked for me but will work for any other golfer. My three kids have always had the patience and humor to be the first ones to try my new methods. Thanks to their willingness and great ability to instantly make changes to their golf swings, I have been able to pre-select the few ideas that have worked great on the three of them before doing further testing with a wider range of players.

I would also like to thank my children for their outstanding idea of taking the photographs included in this book from different and unorthodox angles, which will help the readers to better understand the concepts I will share throughout this book. As we all know, an image is worth a thousand words.

Please note that 100% of the photographs published in this book are original and have not been edited or retouched. Every time you see the golf ball in a photograph, please keep in mind it is the real ball that was captured in real time.

2. BACKGROUND

I was born in Colombia, South America and have been playing golf since I was 11 years old. I grew up playing and still play at the Country Club of Bogota, a traditional club located in the middle of an 8 million people city with a beautiful golf course that has been the host of a Web.com Tour event for the past years.

I was fortunate enough to start playing golf when I was a kid. My friends and I rapidly developed a passion for the game and we had the opportunity to play a lot, practice a lot and compete amongst us. Still, neither of us ever got a chance to play real good golf. For many years, we were all blocked in the upper single digit handicap range, which I believe is very mediocre for anyone who gets the chance to start to play at such a short age.

It was only until my college years that I had a chance to read

David Leadbetter's book "The Golf Swing" that started my interest in learning and understanding the mechanics and fundamentals of a good golf swing. Since then and during the past 25 years, I am confident to say I have read and studied the most important golf instructional books written so far and have analyzed the best players' golf swings in detail.

In my opinion, golf can be the most difficult sport to improve as traditional golf instruction can get too complicated. There are so many pieces in the puzzle, that makes it extremely hard to find the relevant changes needed to improve a golf swing. And even if you find them, it is very difficult to find an easy way to incorporate those changes into your swing.

Through the years, I learned that I have a special ability to understand the key elements of a good golf swing, and to design simple and effective ways for any golfer to incorporate these key elements to their swings.

This has significantly helped my golf game as well. Today I am a scratch player and shoot under par frequently, although I rarely practice my long game and only have time to play once or twice per week.

As golf is my hobby, my sport and my passion, in 2010 I decided to write a golf book that was called: **FINALLY, The Golf Swing's Simple Secret.** A revolutionary method proved for the weekend golfer to significantly improve distance and accuracy from day one.

The book was published on November 2010 and was soon a top seller amongst the more than eight thousand other published golf books and four hundred golf coaching books. For a long time, it was ranked as the 2nd most sold golf book, only behind Ben Hogan's famous Five Lessons: The Modern Fundamentals of Golf book.

This was a very gratifying experience as the majority of golf books are usually written by big names, either players or their coaches.

I never thought I was going to write another golf book until a year ago when I made a major discovery in the short game. More precisely, what I invented is a not a new short game swing, but an incredibly simple, effective and "easy to do" method to do a great short game swing, like the pros, that is almost too good to be true.

If you are looking for a long and complicated book you are in the wrong place. This could be the shortest, less expensive, most concise and best short game golf lesson you may ever receive. And the only reason I confidently say it is because it's simple and it works, period. No doubt that the more you get to practice the technique I am about to teach you, the better you will get, but even if you don't spend long hours on the practice range it should still work and help your short game dramatically.

You don't need to be an Olympic athlete nor have any special physical abilities in order to learn this method and play the short game as the pros. So basically, this book is dedicated to any golfer who wants to improve the short game no matter the skill, age, or gender.

The weekend golfer, who cannot wait until it is Saturday to play, enjoys sharing 18 holes with his friends, and would love to improve but doesn't have the time to practice, nor the interest to learn the mechanical details of the golf swing, will love this method.

This book should also be of great value to the dedicated golfer who is really interested in taking his game to a higher level but has not been able to do so, at least at the pace that he was expecting. He reads golf books and magazines, tries different theories and tips and has more time to practice, but his short game might be struggling or not improving at the rate he wishes or deserves.

Finally, if you are a very skilled player or even a professional who thinks your short game can improve, I seriously suggest you take a look and try this simple method as it may take your game to the next level.

I am aware how frustrating this game can be sometimes and how often you have tried new techniques that have not worked, so I really appreciate you have purchased my book and are willing to try my new method.

Believe me, this time the story can be different. Don't be afraid of implementing the few changes I will ask you to perform; pretty soon you will be surprising your golf partners.

3. INTRODUCTION

Much has been written on the importance of the short game, so I will not spend much time on this. We all know how crucial the short game is in order to make a good score, or at least to not ruin your round. When we think that a PGA tour player misses an average of six greens per round, it's not difficult to estimate how often the rest of us need to pitch, chip or play a bunker shot. For a low handicapper, being able to make a few ups-and-downs in his round can make a huge difference in his score.

For a high handicapper, a good short game will not only have a bigger impact in his score, but it will stop ruining his round because of those typical one or two holes where he bladed a pitch, hit a fat chip or could only get out of the bunker after several attempts.

In my opinion and based on my personal experience, the short game is the hardest part of the game when you don't know how to do it, and the easiest once you learn it. I'm not exaggerating by saying that I have struggled with my short game for more than 25 years while trying every available technique out there. I could say that almost every method that I have tried worked in the practice range, but then in the golf course it only worked for a limited time. Some for a few rounds and some for a few weeks, until suddenly I would badly miss a few short game shots, which immediately made me lose my confidence for that system. Remember, as Bob Rottella said: "Golf is a game of confidence", so once I lost confidence in a method, I couldn't keep using it, and had to continue my search for the short game's holy grail.

Some of the best short game books I have read are Stan Utley's "The Art of Putting/Chipping" and "The Art of Scoring", Dave Stockton's "Unconscious Scoring: Dave Stockton's Guide to Saving Shots Around the Green", Phil Mickelson's "Secrets of the Short Game", Dave Pelz's Short Game Bible: "Master the Finesse Swing and Lower Your Score", and most recently James Sieckmann "Your Short Game Solution: Mastering the Finesse Game from 120 Yards and In". I have also studied in detail the short game chapters of the books written by the best players and coaches in the history of the game including Tiger Woods, Nick Faldo, Jack Nicklaus, David Leadbetter and Butch Harmon.

No one can argue that these great players and coaches have the best understanding of the short game. So having the ability to implement any type of swing taught on these books, the big question I have been asking for several years is: Why did my short game suddenly fail on the golf course or when I was competing after spending so much time practicing it?

A year ago, I found the answer that has opened my mind to a wonderful new approach that you will soon learn. The answer I found was that a short game swing will never be reliable as long as you have to be thinking too much on mechanics during the swing. Unfortunately, when I tried to implement any particular technique without thinking about the mechanics, and only focused on the target, it stopped working. The reason is very simple. The short game swing is not a natural swing. When you look at many pros's short game swings, the club arrives at impact in a different position from where it was at the setup position. In order to achieve this, as well as other movements of the body, arms and hands that happen during the swing, you need to do certain manipulations that are not easy to repeat and will not happen automatically.

There is no doubt that you need to have good mechanics on your short game swing to have good results. Actually, you see several short game swing styles on the PGA. However, there are certain fundamentals and common denominators present in every good swing.

So after more than 20 years of research and testing, I had finally arrived to what I believe is the short game's holy grail concept: In order for a new system to be revolutionary, **I should find a way to make a perfect technique short game swing that looks like the pros and incorporates all of the fundamentals or common denominators of every good short game swing, but without having to think on traditional mechanics during the swing.** Wow, this was certainly not easy to do so I had to start thinking out of the box.

For several months I tried multiple ideas with no spectacular results. I knew how the swing should look like, but I still needed a way to be able to do it without thinking about traditional swing mechanics, or on the swing itself. This goal was not easy to achieve, when you consider that many parts of the body move during a short game swing.

After almost giving up, I decided to study how the brain worked, as I needed to send a message for the body to move the club, arms, hands, shoulders, chest, hips, legs, knees and feet in sync and accordingly to the correct sequence of a short game swing, but without consciously thinking specifically about moving the club or any of these parts of the body. The mind could not interfere with the natural execution of the shot. The mind should not try to control any particular movement of the club or body during the swing.

BINGO! On 2015 I finally came up with a solution that works like magic. **For the first time in the past 20 years, I was lucky to find an incredibly simple, effective, reliable and "easy to do" method that will work for the rest of my life.** I am shooting under par much more frequently than before. I climbed to the first place on the scratch club ranking and was able to stay in this privileged position for a year, ahead of the young players that hit the ball much further and practice and compete much more. I am not afraid of missing a green any more. And most important, I am enjoying the game more than ever before.

Today, I am very excited to share this system with you. As long as you follow the instructions I am about to give you, I am very confident that your short game will improve for a lifetime.

So let's begin…

4. THE PROBLEM TO SOLVE

In my opinion, most good solutions in life are simple. It may take years to find a good solution to a problem. But, when you find it, you may be surprised how simple and almost obvious it was all along.

This short game method was not the exception. It took me 20 years to find the solution that, at the end, was pretty simple and easy to replicate.

Actually, the solution was aimed to solving two different problems:

1. NATURAL SWING WITHOUT MANIPULATIONS: The swing should work with no need to do any manipulations or special maneuvers. In other words, the swing should be and feel natural, in such a way that the club should return to the perfect impact position without trying, or thinking too much.

After several months of testing, I found that the only way to be able to deliver the club to the correct impact position in a natural and consistent manner, was starting the swing from a position where the club was already at the impact position. Plus, this setup position also promotes a great and natural backswing.

So yes, in order to do the swing I will teach you, you will need to do some adjustments to your stance and setup position. Someone may argue that this is part of the swing mechanics and that I was supposed to teach you a method where you didn't have to think of the traditional swing mechanics at all. But this doesn't bother me, because there is a huge difference between thinking about a setup position before you begin the swing, versus thinking about moving a particular part of your body or club during the swing. As long as you don't think too much on traditional mechanics during the swing you should be okay. Specifically, if you don't think about the club, hands, arms, shoulders, chest, hips, knees, legs or feet during the swing, your mind will not interfere with the shot.

In the following chapters, I will explain in detail the adjustments you will need to make to your stance to play the basic chip, pitch, flop and bunker shot.

1. CORRECT BODY AND CLUB MOVEMENT WITHOUT THINKING: The goal was to find a simple way to send a message for the body to move the club, hands, arms, shoulders, chest, hips, legs, knees and feet in sync and accordingly to the correct sequence of a short game swing, but without consciously thinking about moving the club or any of these parts of the body.

To do this, my first step was to understand the fundamentals common in every good short players's swing versus the differences from one style to another. Very interestingly, you find several types of short game swings. Still, there are a few common fundamental movements in every good short game player's swing.

The purpose of this book is to understand what to think and what not to think, in order to perform the proper mechanics of a short swing, instead of thinking about the swing's mechanics.

I will not get too technical on the mechanics of a short swing, but I thought it would be interesting to summarize the main similarities and differences among the best short game players in the world. Please note the following lists are only for informational purposes, you don't need to learn them to do the method I will teach you momentarily:

MAIN DIFFERENCES

- Most of the differences occur on the backswing.
- Some players use a lot of hand action (early wrist set) while other have quiet hands and rely more on body rotation.
- Some players move the club and body in sync during the entire swing while others are more active with the club and upper body and have a more quiet lower body (known as an inverse kinetic chain versus the long game swing).
- Some players take the club back on plane while others pickup the club faster which promotes a steeper plane.
- Some players use the bounce of the wedge more than others.

SIMILARITIES (Common denominators)

- With the exception of the bunker shot, every good short game player has a narrow stance.
- Most good players use a grip for the short game that leans towards the weak side.
- Every good players keeps his center of gravity (lower part of the arc of the swing) from moving back during the backswing.
- Every good player accelerates through impact.
- Every good player keeps turning his body (arms, hips, knees, chest, shoulders) during the entire follow-through.
- Every good players has a well-balanced finish position.

As you can see, my task was much easier now. I was aware that the solution should aim at finding the simplest and most repeatable way for any player of any level, from beginner to professional, to be able to perform a short game swing that included the majority of the common denominators present in every good player's short game swing, while thinking as little as possible.

5.   THE SOLUTION

You're about to read the most important chapter of this book, that will also probably be the most important short game lesson you will ever receive. If you commit yourself to seriously trying this method, I can guarantee that your short game will have a dramatic and significant improvement that will last for the rest of your life. Your swing will start looking very similar to the pros' and you will start hitting crisp and solid shots every time, which is the key for judging distance and leaving the ball close to the pin.

Not only do I use this method myself, but I have tested it on many players with different playing abilities, ages and gender, and I am confident to affirm that it has had incredible results on more than 90% of the cases. Once you understand it and feel it for the first time, it will be very easy to repeat over and over again. Of course, like with everything else in life, the more you practice it, the better you will get and the more confident you will become.

The other great part about it, is that it's just one swing you will learn, that will work for every single short game shot from the 40 yards and in. Of course, you will always have to make adjustments to your stance, ball position, and length of the backswing to perform any particular shot, but you will not have to change the swing technique or swing thoughts. The essence of the swing I will teach you will remain the same from the chip, to the pitch, to the bunker shot.

Once you master this technique, you will love to hit a short game shot and will have a lot of fun doing it. From now on, every time you miss a green you will learn to imagine and visualize the best possible shot. And the greatest part, you will know how to do it and will have all the portfolio of shots available from a pitch-and-run to a flop shot (that should stop quickly) with the same swing technique.

So please pay much attention to the following instructions as they are the key to this new method:

1. STANCE: This should be the easiest part for you to implement. You need to learn that with the exception of the bunker shot, where you need more stability, you should always keep a narrow stance just like the pros do. What I mean by a narrow stance is that the distance between your feet should never be wider than your hips. **As a rule of thumb, the shorter the shot, the narrower the stance should be.**

For a chip shot around the green, the feet should be slightly separated (approx. 2 to 3 inches), while for a 30 yard pitch shot the separation should be as wide as your hips. As a bunker shot usually requires a longer swing, the separation should be similar to a long shot, which as a reference you can consider using the width of your shoulders. As your left foot should be slightly open, which means it should be pointing slightly to the left to promote a good body rotation on the follow-through, the width of the feet I just explained should be taken from the middle of the feet and not from the toes.

Please note that although it's pretty simple to keep a narrow stance, it's something you should always remember to do, as the mechanics and body movement of a good short game will not work with a wide stance.

I also recommend using a very slightly open stance, which means your two feet should aim a little to the left of parallel to the ball-to-target line. If a club was placed in front of your right toes and parallel to the ball-to-target line, your left toes should be slightly separated from the club (picture 1). Your stance should look similar to your long shot stance with the exception that it should be narrower and a bit open. Even if you don't open your stance you should be fine as long as it is narrow.

Picture 1. Optimal narrow and slightly open stance

I do not recommend using a very open stance as it is confusing to know where the back, middle and front of your stance are when your two feet are turned to the left too much. For example, imagine you have the ball in front of your right toes which makes you believe the ball is in the back of your stance. However, as the center of the arc is determined by the heels of your feet and not the toes, this ball only appeared to be on the back while in reality it was in the middle of your stance. I don't want to confuse you with this explanation which at the end is not very relevant. **What is really relevant is to ensure that you always know where the back, middle and front of your stance is, as the ball should always be in one of these three spots depending on the type of shot you want to hit. And the best way to do this right is by having a square or slightly open stance.** In the following chapter I will use photographs to show you the correct stance for each particular shot, so you don't need to worry about the details at this point.

Remember when we mentioned that we wanted to start the swing with the club at the impact position so we could get to the same position on the down-swing without the need of manipulations? Well, this is where we learn to do it, and it is very simple. Once you decide the type of shot you are hitting, you step to the ball, take your stance, **and only grip the club once the club shaft is in the position you want it to be at the impact position.** Keep in mind that the shaft position will change depending on the type of shot you want to hit. You can also decide if you start with the club face square or open to the target, which will further affect your ball flight and spin. All these adjustments will be explained with photographs in the following chapters, so don't worry about understanding it yet.

Up to now, all you need to know is that: i) your stance should be narrow, ii) your stance should be slightly open, iii) your ball position should always be in the back, middle or front of your stance, iv) your club shaft should start at the same position you want it to be at impact, and you should only grip the club once it's in this desired position, v) your club face could start square to the target or open, and vi) you need to adjust these variables on every short game shot depending on the type of shot you plan to hit (chip, low pitch, normal pitch, flop shot, etc).

I will show you the perfect stance and the adjustments needed in detail in the following chapters.

2. BACKSWING: This goal was a little more complicated to achieve. I needed to find a simple way to move and turn correctly during the backswing without thinking about the club, hands, arms, shoulders, hips or legs, and without moving the center of gravity back. **As a matter of fact, the best short game players in the world slightly move their center of gravity, or lower point of their swing arc, towards the target during the backswing. It is important to note that staying still or frozen during the backswing like a putting stroke is a big mistake that will lead to thin, fat or mis-hit shots. The body needs to turn and move naturally during the backswing while moving the center of the arc slightly towards the target.** This is the key of a great short game backswing.

The solution was pretty obvious. **All you need to do is to stop focusing on the the club, hands, arms, shoulders, hips or legs, and just think of gradually transferring your weight to your left foot during the backswing.**

As I will explain in the next chapter, I would recommend to start your short game swing with your weight distributed equally on both feet (50% each). By the end of the backswing, your weight should be approximately 67% (two thirds) on you left foot and 33% (one third) on your right foot. Actually, your head could eventually move a bit towards your left side during the backswing, although you should not think about this.

No matter if you hinge your hands or not, if you have a steeper or shallower swing plane or what type of shot you are hitting, thinking of gradually transferring your weight to your left foot during the backswing will ensure that you turn correctly without moving your center of gravity back.

I suggest you stop reading for a moment and try to do this inverse weight transfer I just explained, simulating a backswing without holding a club. At the beginning, it may feel a little awkward as you want your weight to be gradually moving towards your left foot while the club is moving in the other direction. But very soon, you will start to feel this movement very natural and easy to do.

As a check-point, during the backswing you will notice that if you do it correctly, your left knee should move slightly forward (Sequence 1). However, if you are not transferring your weight to the left foot during the backswing as you are supposed to, you will notice that your left knee will move forward right instead of just forward (Sequence 2).

Please keep in mind that this is just a check-point you can use to confirm if you are doing it right, but you should never think about voluntarily moving the knees.

Remember that the key during the backswing is to focus only

on gradually transferring your weight to your left foot without thinking about the club, hands, arms, shoulders, hips, knees, legs or feet.

You will be surprised on how well the body and club move automatically during the backswing without thinking about anything else rather than transferring your weight towards your left foot.

Sequence 1. Correct knee forward motion that occurs when you transfer your weight to the left during the backswing.

- Remember to have a narrow stance before starting this backswing drill with no club.

- Look at the slight forward motion of the left knee when doing your backswing.

- The knee forward movement is a consequence of the weight transfer to the left side during the backswing.

- This should only be used as a check point as you should not think of the knees.

 Sequence 2. Incorrect knee forward and right motion that occurs when you do not transfer your weight to the left during the backswing.

- Look at the slight forward and right motion of the left knee as a consequence of not transferring your weight to the left foot during the backswing.

- This should only be used as a check point as you should not be thinking about the knees.

As a matter of fact, this weight transfer to the left during the backswing is very subtle and difficult to notice when looking at a pro's short game swing.

When looked at from a face on view, it will appear as if the player is staying still although you can see him turning. However, if you compare the initial setup position versus the position attained at the end of the short game backswing, you will notice this slight transfer of weight to the left side (Sequence 3).

Sequence 3. Weight transfer to the left during the backswing

- When comparing the following two positions, your first impression could be that I am staying very still.

- However, if you look carefully you will be able to notice the slight transfer of weight to the left during the backswing.

1. DOWNSWING AND FOLLOW-THROUGH: Finally, the most important part of the short game swing is the downswing and follow-through. Remember that every good short game player accelerates through impact, keeps turning his body (arms, hips, knees, chest, shoulders) during the entire follow-through, and has a well-balanced finish position.

The solution I found was very simple to do and has incredibly amazing results. Once i) the setup is correct for the shot to be played, and ii) you slightly move your weight towards the target during the backswing, **all you have to think of during the downswing and follow-through is to follow the ball with your eyes until it comes to a complete stop.**

Even though it may sound hard to believe, the "don't move your eyes" tip is a great paradigm for the short game, that ensures you will do it wrong. **Meanwhile, just focusing on following the ball with your eyes from the moment it is struck until it comes to a complete stop, guarantees you will accelerate through impact, make a perfect follow-through turn and finish your swing with a perfectly balanced position.**

In other words, following the ball with your eyes, seeing it fly, roll and stop is very easy to do and makes your short game swing look just like the pros. You will be amazed on how fluid and great your swing will look and feel; and how crisp you will start hitting every shot.

If your mind is focused on following the ball with your eyes, it will eliminate any intentional movements of any parts of your body, which will eliminate any unnatural manipulations that cause thin, fat and bad shots due to an uncoordinated or decelerating swing. **Please note that following the ball with your eyes is different from taking your eyes away from the ball abruptly.** You should always be looking at the ball.

From the beginning of the swing until the impact, your eyes should be looking down to the ball. From that instant on, your eyes should follow the ball. The mastery of this technique will ensure you are able to see the ball the entire way. This smooth and delicate movement of the eyes following the ball from the moment it leaves the clubhead is what guarantees that you will hit it solidly every time, as it will make you turn correctly, smoothly and with the perfect kinetic sequence.

So now that you have learned the basic stance, backswing and follow-through method that I have just explained, I invite you to move to the next chapter to analyze and learn the details of each specific shot, one at a time.

6. THE CHIP SHOT

The chip shot is one of the easiest shots to hit. It is a very short shot that should only be played when your are very close to the green, no more than a few yards away. The ball should fly the least amount possible, in order to land on the green and start rolling towards the hole. Although you should do a very subtle weight transfer to the left during the backswing, the swing is so small that it may look more like a putting stroke with a follow through. The key to this shot is to have a descending blow with the shaft leaning forward at the impact position, which should occur naturally without any type of manipulations as we will start the swing with the club already set at this shaft leaning forward position.

You can use any club from an eight iron to a gap-wedge. Unless you have a very short chip with not much green to work with, when you may want to play a sand-wedge to have less roll, I recommend you always use the same chipping club to get a better feel for distance. I try to play most of my chip shots with my pitching wedge. Keep in mind that because of the big forward lean of the shaft at the setup and impact position, the pitching wedge (or any club you use) will be significantly de-lofted. My pitching wedge at impact may have the dynamic loft of an eight iron.

The Chip Stance

Particularly to the chip shot and to guarantee a descending blow and a good contact, you should place the ball on your right side and your hands and grip on your left side.

The feet should be slightly separated (only 2 to 3 inches) and the club face should be square to the target. For increased touch and distance control, I suggest you hold the club further down the grip and with a very light grip pressure.

Once you know where to aim, I recommend you follow this three step setup routine to obtain a perfect chip stance (Sequence 4):

Sequence 4. Chip shot setup routine

1. Hold your club with your right hand. Take a very narrow and slightly open stance (your feet should not be separated by more than 2 to 3 inches). Your right foot should be perpendicular to the target and pointing directly to the ball. Place your clubhead behind the ball.

2. With your right hand, move the club grip until it is in front of you left thigh.

3. Grip the club with both hands from that position. It is very important that you do not hold your grip with two hands before the grip is in front of your left thigh. This is the key to achieving the same shaft lean at impact position.

The following photograph will help you understand how a correct chip posture and stance should look and feel like.

Picture 2. Chip setup position from the player's perspective

The Chip Swing

Once you are ready to make the shot, verify that your weight is distributed 50% on each foot. Then, all you need to do and think of is to:

1. Gradually transfer your weight to your left foot during the backswing. As the backswing is so short on the chip shot, you would actually be doing a minimum, very subtle weight transfer.

2. Focus deeply and only on following the ball with your eyes from the moment it leaves the clubhead until it comes to a complete stop. This will guarantee you accelerate through impact, make a perfect follow-through turn and finish your swing with a balanced position.

For the chip shot, the only change you will need to make to hit a longer or shorter shot is to adjust the length of the backswing. However, this is something that should happen automatically without having to think about it.

Sequence 5. Chip swing from a face-on view

- Notice how my eyes always follow the ball.

- The club always stays low both in the backswing and in the follow-through. This is only a consequence of starting the swing with the ball back and shaft leaning so much towards the left.

The beauty of this system is that I didn't need to make any changes to my swing thoughts to keep the club low. It's only a consequence of the stance.

Sequence 5. Chip swing from a face-on view

Sequence 6. Chip swing from the target view

Sequence 6. Chip swing from the target view

- My eyes always follow the ball, which keeps me turning during the entire follow-through.

- Look at how low the ball flies even though this was a long chip swing, again only as a consequence of the setup position.

7.   THE LOW PITCH

The low pitch is similar to the chip shot. The main difference is that you want to hit it further and don't want to hit it as low as the chip shot. Thus, you will still play the ball on your right foot but your stance will be a little wider for more stability, and the club doesn't have to be leaning so much to the left.

Out of the three pitch shots I will teach you (low pitch, normal pitch and high pitch or flop shot), I would say this is the easiest to hit and the one you should use the most, as it has a bigger margin for error. The only reason you cannot use this type of shot all the time is that you need plenty of green to work with as the ball will fly lower and roll towards the target. This explains why pros always prefer not to miss the shots to the green on the short side.

This shot can be used from the 40 yards and in, until you are so close to the green that you would prefer the chip shot. The ball should also fly the least amount possible to land on the green and start rolling towards the hole. The key to this shot is to have the ball behind (to the right side) of your center of gravity, or lowest point of the arc, so that you will never hit it fat. This again occurs naturally without any type of manipulations as we will start the swing with the club already set at the desired impact position.

You can use a gap, sand or lob wedge for this shot. I like to play most of my low pitch shots with my 58 degrees sand-wedge. Although it has 58 degrees, the ball will fly lower due to the stance and set position. The forward lean of the shaft at the setup and impact position will de-loft your sand-wedge.

The Low Pitch Stance

I will keep emphasizing and repeating that a great part of the key to success of this method is having a good stance according to the desired shot, as the only way to deliver the club at the perfect impact position, without swing manipulations, is by starting the swing from a position where the club is already at that impact position.

For the pitch shot stance, place the ball on the right side and the club face square to the target. The club shaft will be leaning towards the left but not as much as for the chip as we want the hands and grip to start at the center of your stance. We will still be having a descending blow, hitting the ball with the leading edge of the wedge instead of the bounce. For increased touch and distance control, you may want to use a light grip pressure.

Once you know where to aim, I recommend you follow this two step setup routine to obtain a perfect stance (Sequence 7):

Sequence 7. Low pitch setup routine

1. Hold your club with your right hand. Take a narrow and slightly open stance (not as narrow as the stance used for the chip shot). Your right foot should be perpendicular to the target and pointing directly to the ball. Place your clubhead behind the ball.

2. As your grip should already be in the middle of your body, which is its natural position, all you need to do is grip the club with both hands. It is very important that you do not hold your grip with two hands before the grip is in the middle of your body. This is the key to achieving the same shaft lean at impact position.

Picture 3. Low pitch setup position from the player's perspective

The Low Pitch Swing

Once you are ready to make the shot, verify that your weight is distributed 50% on each foot.

Then, all you need to do and think is:

Note: *As one of the main benefits of this system is to use the same swing for all shots, the following two instructions will be the same for the chip, pitch, flop and bunker shots:*

1. Gradually transfer your weight to your left foot during the backswing. A good reference would be to have two thirds of your weight on your left foot and one third on your right foot by the time you finish your backswing.

1.Focus only on following the ball with your eyes from the moment it leaves the clubhead until it comes to a complete stop. This will guarantee you accelerate through impact, make a perfect follow-through turn and finish your swing with a balanced position.

You can change the distance you want the ball to travel by changing the club and/or the length of the backswing. However, this last one will happen automatically without having to think about it.

Sequence 8. Low pitch swing from a face-on view

- See how my eyes always follow the ball.

- The club always stays low as a consequence of starting the swing with the ball back and the shaft leaning to the left. Another way to see this is by looking at the extension of the arms that continue immediately after impact.

My two swing thoughts remain the same, so you don't have to think about the extension of the arms and club or about anything else.

Sequence 8. Low pitch swing from a face-on view

Sequence 9. Low pitch swing from the target view

Sequence 9. Low pitch swing from the target view

- My eyes always follow the ball which keeps me turning during the entire follow-through.

- Look how low the ball flies and how low the club stays as a consequence of the setup position.

- Looking from this view you can see that the clubhead stays outside of the hands during the follow-through, due to the initial leaning of the club.

The last two comment are for informational purposes only, as the changes between the different shots occur only because of the different stances. The swing is the same.

Sequence 10. Low pitch swing from a diagonal view

- From this angle you can see how synced is the body turn during the entire follow-through, achieved just by transferring your weight to the left during the backswing and following the ball with your eyes.

Sequence 10. Low pitch swing from a diagonal view

8. THE NORMAL PITCH

The normal pitch is a comfortable approach shot you want to use when you neither have enough green to play a low pitch, nor too little green which would require a flop shot. It can be used all around the green, as the ball will get some relevant altitude but will not roll too much.

The ball will be played from the middle of your stance, which is exactly the center of your swing and lower part of your arc.

You can use a sand or lob wedge for this shot. I like to play most of my normal pitch shots with my 60 degrees sand-wedge. I like the 60 degrees because the ball will generate more spin, thus will check a bit on the green, which gives me more control.

The Normal Pitch Stance

The ball will be played from the center of the stance and you will want the club shaft to be vertical (with no shaft lean), both at the start and at the impact position.

I recommend you take your normal grip with the club face slightly open, as this will add a little bounce to your club, which will increase your margin for error and forgiveness.

Once you know where to aim, I recommend you follow this two step setup routine to obtain a perfect stance (Sequence 11).

Sequence 11. Normal pitch setup routine

1. Hold your club with your right hand. Take a narrow and slightly open stance (your feet should not be separated by more than your hip width). The ball should be in the middle of your stance. Place your clubhead behind the ball.

2. As your grip should already be in the middle of your body right in front of your zipper, all you need to do is grip the club with both hands, preferably with the club head slightly open.

The following photograph will help you understand how a correct posture and stance for the normal pitch should look and feel like.

Picture 4. Normal pitch setup position from the player's perspective

The Normal Pitch Swing

Once you are ready to make the shot, verify that your weight is distributed 50% on each foot.

Then, all you need to do and think about is to:

Note: *As one of the main benefits of this system is to use the same swing for all shots, the following two instructions will be the same for the chip, pitch, flop and bunker shots:*

1. Gradually transfer your weight to your left foot during the backswing. A good reference would be to have two thirds of your weight on your left foot and one third on your right foot by the time you finish your backswing.

1. Focus only on following the ball with your eyes from the moment it leaves the clubhead until it comes to a complete stop. This will guarantee you accelerate through impact, make a perfect follow-through turn and finish your swing with a balanced position.

You can change the distance you want the ball to travel by changing the length of the backswing. This will happen automatically without having to think about it.

Sequence 12. Normal pitch swing from a face-on view

- My eyes always follow the ball no matter the shot I am hitting.

- You can notice the club shaft arriving at impact position at the exact same position it was at address.

Sequence 12.
Normal pitch
swing from a face-
on view

Sequence 13.
Normal pitch
swing from the
target view

Sequence 13. Normal pitch swing from the target view

- The ball has mid trajectory, as a consequence of the setup position.

- Looking at the last frame you can notice the clubshaft position at the end of the swing is centered right in the middle of the chest between both arms, just as it was at the beginning of the swing.

<u>Again:</u> These are all comments for informational purposes as all these changes between the different shots occur automatically and only because of the different stances. The swing is the same.

Sequence 14. Normal pitch swing from a diagonal view

- From this angle you can see how synced is the body turn during the entire follow-through by just thinking about transferring your weight to the left during the backswing and following the ball with the eyes.

- Looking at the last frame, you can notice that the club ends higher than the chip and the low pitch, as consequence of the vertical shaft (no shaft lean) at the setup position.

Sequence 14.
Normal pitch swing
from a diagonal
view

9. THE FLOP PITCH

The lob shot or flop shot is a high pitch shot that travels a short distance and lands softly on the green stopping with very little roll. This is the shot you need to hit when you miss the green on the short side and have to carry a bunker to a green that has very little room to work with.

People are usually afraid of hitting this shot, which is understandable, as without having the proper technique it is very easy to blade it or hit it fat. I am confident to say that with the technique I have been teaching you throughout this book, and with the correct stance I will explain to you momentarily, you will be surprised on how easy it is to hit this shot.

You should use your lob wedge for this shot. I like to play most of my flop shots with my 60 degrees sand-wedge which is the most lofted club I have on my bag. I also hold the club with the face open and vary how much I open it depending on how high I need to hit it and how fast I need to stop it.

The Flop Shot Stance

The ball will be played from the left side of the stance but you still want the club shaft to be vertical (with no shaft lean) thus you will need to move the grip towards your left thigh before you grip the club.

Remember to open the club face (before you grip the club), as this will add loft to the club and the ball will fly higher and land softer.

Once you know where to aim, I recommend you follow this three step setup routine to obtain a perfect stance (Sequence 15).

 Sequence 15. Flop shot setup routine

1. Hold your club with your right hand. Take a narrow and slightly open stance (your feet should not be separated by more than your hip width). The ball should be in front of your left foot. Place your clubhead behind the ball.

2. With your right hand, move the club grip until it is in front of you left thigh.

3. Grip the club with both hands from that position. It is very important that you do not hold your grip with two hands before the grip is in front of your left thigh. This is the key to achieving the same shaft lean at impact position.

The following photograph will help you understand how a correct flop shot posture and stance should look and feel like.

Picture 5. Flop shot setup position from the player's perspective

The Flop Shot Swing

Once you are ready to make the shot, verify that your weight is distributed 50% on each foot. Then, all you need to do and think about is to:

Note: *As one of the main benefits of this system is to use the same swing for all shots, the following two instructions will be the same for the chip, pitch, flop and bunker shots:*

1. Gradually transfer your weight to your left foot during the backswing. A good reference would be to have two thirds of your weight on your left foot and one third on your right foot by the time you finish your backswing.

1. Focus only on following the ball with your eyes from the moment it leaves the clubhead until it comes to a complete stop. This will guarantee you accelerate through impact, make a perfect follow-through turn and finish your swing with a balanced position.

Specifically for the Flop Shot: You can change the distance you want the ball to travel by changing the the length of the backswing **and by changing the amount you open the club face. The more you open it, the higher and shorter the ball will travel, thus the ball will have less roll.**

Sequence 16. Flop shot swing from a face-on view

- My eyes always follow the ball, no matter how high the ball flies.

- Notice how my center of gravity, or lower point of the swing, is always behind the ball due to the ball position on the left side of my stance.

- A typical characteristic of this shot is having the club pointing to the sky at the finish position.

<u>Once Again:</u> These two last comments for informational purposes as all these changes between the different shots occur automatically and only because of the different stances. The swing is the same.

Sequence 16. Flop shot swing from a face-on view

Sequence 17. Flop shot swing from the target view

Sequence 17. Flop shot swing from the target view

- My eyes always follow the ball which keeps me turning during the entire follow-through.

- Check how quickly the ball gets up in the air.

Sequence 18. Flop shot shot swing from a diagonal view

Sequence 18. Flop shot shot swing from a diagonal view

9. THE BUNKER SHOT

The bunker shot may be the shot that scares most amateurs. On the other hand, you hear many tour players saying it could be the easiest shot to play as there is more margin for error. I agree that without knowing how to do it, falling on a bunker can ruin your round. You may have trouble getting out in one shot, or even worse, you can blade it 50 yards over the green.

However, the good news is that once you learn how to play the bunker shot you will find it easy to get the ball on the green and may even start to get disappointed when you don't leave it close to the pin. The other great part of my system is that you don't need to learn a different swing technique for the bunker.

Like in any other short game shot, it is important at the bunker to accelerate through impact, make a perfect follow-through turn, and finish your swing in a perfectly balanced position. As you have already learned by now, these three requirements to hit a good short game are achieved by transferring your weight to the left during the backswing and following the ball with your eyes until it comes to a complete stop. However, in order for this method to work like magic, when hitting from the sand, you will also need to make some important adjustments to your stance and ball position that I will explain momentarily.

Before I go into the details, let me share with you a few golden rules of a bunker shot that will help you understand the reasons for the stance adjustments I will ask you to do:

BUNKER SHOT GOLDEN RULES

1. You hit the sand, not the ball: This may sound obvious as we all know we should hit the sand behind the ball so that the club will slide underneath the ball pushing the sand and the ball out of the bunker and onto the green. Still, most amateurs take their stance placing the clubhead immediately behind the ball, instead of placing the ball 1.5 to 3 inches ahead of the clubhead. This is a big mistake that will force the player to manipulate the swing, as he now needs the clubhead to hit the sand 1.5 to 3 inches behind his setup or natural position.

2. You should never blade it: In a pitch or chip shot you may occasionally hit the ball a little thin with the clubhead coming through impact just above the ground, and still hit a good shot. In the bunker, this same slight miss will be the kiss of death as the ball could fly well past the green, due to the length of the swing. Therefore, we should always dig our feet in the sand before hitting the shot as this will lower the arc of the swing to ensure you will not blade it.

3. You should use the bounce of the club: The amount of bounce in a sand-wedge is defined as how much lower is the lowest point of the sole in relation to the leading edge. I don't want to get too technical on this. The important aspect to understand is that bounce is your friend as it helps reduce the resistance of the sand when hitting behind the ball, avoiding the club to dig. As a rule of thumb, a standard sand-wedge with 10 or 12 degrees of bounce should be just perfect. The key issue I want to share with you is that you can change the effective bounce by changing the position of the club shaft and club face. You should never want the club shaft to lean forward (like we do with the chip shot or low pitch), as this will decrease the effective bounce and cause the club to dig. Your club shaft should be vertical at the setup and impact position. Also, closing the club face will decrease effective bounce so you should always play a bunker shot with the club face open.

4. You control your distance with the loft: As you remember, with the chip and pitch shots we controlled the distance mainly by adjusting the length of the backswing. In the bunker shot it is somehow different. Although you could end up doing a bigger backswing for a longer bunker shot versus a shorter one, making a small backswing on a bunker shot can be very dangerous. Thus, the best and easiest way to control distance is by changing the loft of your sand-wedge. You do this by changing the club you play and by changing the amount you open your club face at address. The higher the loft the less it will travel and vice versa. You can open the club face just a little for a normal or long bunker shot, and you can open it a great amount if you have a shorter shot, when you need the ball to fly less and stop faster. For example, I play my normal bunker shot with my 58 degrees sand-wedge and my club face somewhat open. For a longer shot, I will use my same 58 with the club face slightly open, (not as open as for the normal distance sand-wedge shot) or I may use my 52 degrees sand-wedge. For a shorter bunker shot, I will either use my 58 degrees with the club face very open or my 60 degrees sand wedge with the face very open as well. Just keep in mind that you do not want to open the club face too much when there is not enough sand, as the added bounce will have no room to slide under the ball, which will cause the club to bounce and blade the ball.

With these principals in mind, let's move on to the stance

checkpoints.

The Bunker Shot Stance

As the posture of the bunker shot is somehow similar to the long shot, I didn't find it necessary to include a setup routine. Instead, I will list the five key points you need to have so you can use it as a check-list:

1. Use a wider and slightly open stance, and dig your feet into the sand. I recommend that the width of your stance be similar to the width of your shoulders.

2. Grip the club with the club face open.

3. Position your hands and club face right in the middle of your stance so the shaft stays perpendicular to the ground with no shaft lean.

4. Make sure the ball is between 1.5 to 3 inches ahead of your club. The closer you hit to the ball, the more spin and less roll you will get. The further behind you hit from the ball, the less spin, more roll, and more margin for error you will get.

5. Verify that your weight is distributed 50% on each foot. In case you have an uphill or downhill lie, you should incline your body according to the ground inclination so your weight before starting the backswing is still distributed 50% on each foot.

Pictures 6 and 7. Bunker shot stance

The Bunker Shot Swing

Once you are ready to make the shot, verify that your weight is distributed 50% on each foot.

Then, all you need to do and think about is to:

Note: *As one of the main benefits of this system is to use the same swing for all shots, the following two instructions will be the same for the chip, pitch and bunker shots:*

1. Gradually transfer your weight to your left foot during the backswing. A good reference would be to have two thirds of your weight on your left foot and one third on your right foot by the time you finish your backswing.

2. Focus only on following the ball with your eyes from the moment it leaves the clubhead until it comes to a complete stop. This will guarantee you accelerate through impact, make a perfect follow-through turn and finish your swing with a balanced position.

Specifically for the Bunker Shot: Very important, you should look at the ball from the beginning of the swing, and not the sand. This may feel a little strange the first time you do it as the ball is 1.5 to 3 inches ahead of the club face. But this is key in order to be able to follow the ball once it leaves the sand.

Sequence 19. Bunker shot from a face-on view (a)

- The club head is approximately 2 inches behind the ball at the address position.

- Check the club pointing at the sky at the finish position, as a consequence of the club shaft being vertical (no shaft lean) at the setup position.

Remember changes between the different shots occur automatically and only because of the different stances. The swing is the same.

Sequence 19.
Bunker shot from a
face-on view (a)

Sequence 20.
Bunker shot from a
face-on view (b)

Sequence 20. Bunker shot from a face-on view (b)

- Notice the slight weight transfer to the left during the backswing.

- The club head gets past the ball after impact, which is a characteristic of a good bunker shot. Keep in mind, this is not noticeable or something you should be thinking of when hitting the ball.

Sequence 21. Bunker shot from the target view.

- See how my eyes follow the ball; the bunker is no exception to this important rule.

Sequence 21. Bunker shot from the target view.

10. CONCLUSION

I hope you have enjoyed this book and are looking forward to trying, practicing and implementing my short game method as soon as possible. I am confident that if you dedicate some time to master it, your short game will have an incredible improvement and you will start making shots you had only dreamed of making until now.

The biggest challenge that you may face now is breaking the paradigms that we have incorrectly been taught for so many years, like "transferring your weight back", "staying still during the backswing" or "keeping your eyes on the ground during the follow-through".

As long as you believe in this method and are willing to give it an honest try, I have no doubt you will end up agreeing it is so simple, effective and "easy to do", that is almost too good to be true.

Good luck!

11. LONG GAME

The long game requires a different technique that I will not be able to cover here, as this book was only about the short game.

In case you are interested in improving your long game as well, I invite you to read my book **FINALLY: THE GOLF SWING'S SIMPLE SECRET** - A revolutionary method proved for the weekend golfer to significantly improve distance and accuracy from day one.

If you have ever wondered why the average handicap on the USGA has barely improved in the last 20 years? The answer is very simple:

a. Most of the players have not improved their short or long game.

b. The golf swing is very difficult to understand and to perform.

c. The average weekend golfer would love to improve but doesn´t have the time or the interest to spend long hours practicing.

In this book, I will share with you a revolutionary method proved for the weekend golfer of any level to significantly improve distance and accuracy from day one, based on three main principles:

1. FOCUS ON CHANGES THAT MOST POSITIVELY AFFECT RESULTS: Opposite to the traditional methods, this book will only ask you to make changes in the most relevant parts of the swing needed to hit solid and consistent shots: the backswing and the transition between the backswing and the downswing.

2. LEARN HOW TO DEVELOP AN EASY, REPEATABLE AND SOLID BACKSWING: One of the biggest breakthroughs of the method was the development of a unique and much easier way to consistently make a solidly sound backswing that will look similar to the Tiger Wood's one plane backswing he used during his best years, but much simpler to learn, to do and to repeat.

3. LEARN HOW TO CREATE LAG: Being able to increase lag during the downswing is one of the major differences between the amateur's golf swing versus a professional's and probably one of the most misunderstood concepts of golf. In this book you will easily learn how to lag the club like the pros, dramatically improving your clubhead speed, ball striking ability and distance.

END

46639595R00068

Made in the USA
San Bernardino, CA
11 March 2017